Richard Ridyard

LOWTON

- A Bygone Era -

Edited by Peter Riley

P & D Riley

First published in 1935 as Memories of Lowton
This edited, re-titled edition first published 1998

P & D Riley
12 Bridgeway East,
Cheshire,
WA7 6LD

This edition © by P & D Riley

ISBN: 1 874712 40 9

British Library Cataloguing in Publication Data
A catalogue Record for this book is available from the British Library

Printed in England

Introduction

T he work of Richard Ridyard first appeared in 1935 under the title **Memories of Lowton** and was republished again under the same title in 1979 and 1993 in an A5 format without the benefit of many illustrations, and it was not our intention to republish the book again for several more years. However, fate intervened, and we received numerous requests to provide an ever eager public with a brief history book about Lowton so we decided to use Mr. Ridyard's excellent book in an edited format and brighten it up with numerous illustrations. This book is the result.

It follows the same format of several other popular titles published by ourselves and so we naturally hope it will be well received by local people and visitors to Lowton alike. For a small area Lowton has a remarkably interesting and long history, and this edition will, I am sure, be a catalyst for anyone interested in the area to follow through with a more detailed study of their own, and for visitors a sufficient tasting of what Lowton has had to offer throughout the centuries. But whatever the reason for buying this book it is sincerely hoped it will be enjoyed.

Peter Riley

Acknowledgements

The publishers offer grateful thanks to the following for their invaluable help in making this publication possible.

Les Florey of Lane Head News in Lowton.

The late Bert Worsley, a true lover of Lowton's history.

Peter Worsley, Bert's son, for permission to use his father's photographs,

Alan Nixon of Annex Copy Shops in Golborne.

One

Although it is almost 50 years since I left my native village of Lowton, I still love to have an occasional ramble through its highways and by-ways, and meditate on the happy boy and young manhood days I had during the 24 years I lived in one of the two old cottages, still standing in Hesketh Meadow Lane. It was during a recent ramble through the village, and while thinking of the changes that have taken place during the past 60 years, that I resolved to write all that I could learn of its history, and record my own recollections, and the reminiscences of other people, which have been kindly loaned to me.

That Lowton stands on high ground, compared with the surrounding district, is seen from the ordnance levels which are as follows:-Lane Head, which is about the centre of the township, is 130 feet above sea level. St. Luke's Church, 128 feet. The boundary at Lowton Junction, 124 feet. St. Mary's Church, 120 feet. Boundary, near Shepherd's Inn, 87 feet. The Flash, 75 feet ,and the highway at Pennington Brook Bridge, 71 feet.

Knowing the above facts, I had often wondered why an area, situated on comparatively high ground had been given the name Lowon, or Low-Town. Had it been on low-lying land the name could have been easily understood. Aware that some districts derive their name from ancient families of land owners, I at first thought that this might be the case with Lowton, and in my research I found that the earliest reference to Lowton is in an old Culcheth Deed, undated, but probably of the 13th century.

The origin of the word "Low" is a corruption of "Llaw" which means a hill or undulating ground, and has thus the very opposite meaning of our word "Low" and Lowton rightly interpreted is Llawton, or Hilltown. Werneth Low, near Oldham, Bucklow, near Knutsford in Cheshire, are other examples.

The area of the township is 1,830 acres, and the population, according to the 1931 census, 3,857. One hundred years ago the population was about 2,000. The earliest reliable history relative to the Parish, like most other districts, centres round the Parish Church.

Although Parishes were first formed in England about the year 636, it is not until 1732 that we learn much about the beginnings of Lowton as a parish. It is recorded that St. Oswald, a Christian Prince of Northumbria had a palace in the district at the time parishes began to be formed and as Winwick Church bears his name, it is reasonable to suppose that Winwick Parish was formed shortly after his death. It then included Lowton, Newton, Golborne, Kenyon, Culcheth, Earlestown, Wargrave and Ashton.

At the time the church was erected, Lowton would indeed be a remote and sequestered village, and most of the inhabitants would no doubt be engaged in pastoral and agricultural pursuits. It is possible to visualize something of the topography of the township from an old plan of the district and two acts of Parliament passed in 1761-3, which I have been privileged to peruse and make extracts. One of these acts of Parliament refers to the necessary improvement of the main roads, beginnning near Bolton, and leading through Chowbent, Leigh, Lowton and Parr Stocks, near St. Helens.

For the slow horse-drawn traffic of the period the roads would be ideal and when I was a boy the length of road extending through Lowton was much in the same condition as when finished by the trustees one hundred years previous. About 60 years ago the cobble stones were taken up, broken into pieces and relaid as watered macadam, dressed curb stones substituted for the large cobbled ones, and the toll house and gates, which for one hundred years had stood at Lane Head, were taken down. The name given on the old plan for the road through Lowton is Peel Ditch Lane, but in process of time it became changed to Mather Lane in honour of the Mather family, who at one time lived in a cottage which stood near the original road between Lowton Common and Lane Head. The road is now known as Newton Road.

Cottages in Hesketh Meadow Lane, close to where the author was born

Immediately after the Turnpike Road had been reconstructed merchandise began to be conveyed in carts between the manufacturing towns of Bolton, Blackburn and Bury, etc., and the market towns of Warrington and Liverpool. Stage coaches also ran upon the road until the advent of railways. The whole of the Common, Heath and Waste Land, was held by about 80 occupiers: the Common, lying between what is now Church Lane and the district boundary at Pennington, and the Heath, was in the area between Church Lane and Lowton Junction.

The origin of the names given to most of the roads is easy to understand. Common Lane was the lane across the Common, and Heath Lane would cross the land on which the heather grew. Byrom Lane would be named after the Byrom family who at one time resided at Byrom Hall. How Stone Cross Lane came by its name I have not been able to find out with any degree of certainty, but there is a belief strongly held by the old folks living in the district that one time a stone cross stood at the junction of the roads near to where St. Lukes Church now stands.

That such a belief is feasible, is the knowledge that in France and other Catholic countries there are to be seen many crosses erected by the road sides, and it is reasonable to suppose that in the days when Catholicism held sway in this country many crosses would be erected giving place names to districts such as Cross Hillock,

Taking a break from baling on Byrom's farm were (l to r) Eddie Lee, Harry Aaron, Albert Wild and Harold Eckersley

Astley, Cross Lane, Salford, and Stubshaw Cross, Ashton-in-Makerfield. During the turbulent period of the Civil War in the 17th century most of the crosses would be demolished, the one that gave the name of Stone Cross Lane, among them.

From an agricultural standpoint it is interesting to know of the varied quality of the land which comprises the township. Clay underlies most of the area between Church Lane and Lowton Common, and this part of the Parish has always been best suited for grass and pasturage for cattle. In the area extending from Church Lane to the boundary of the Township at Lowton Junction, the subsoil is of a sandy nature and it has been the custom to grow rotation crops of potatoes, wheat and oats, etc., and the district has produced some of the best ploughmen in the county.

During a recent ramble over the west end of the township, I was informed by a native with whom I had lengthy conversation, that there was still a fair amount of both ground and winged game in the neighbourhood, and he stated that he had seen that day a hare run across the field in which we were standing, and on the previous Saturday a party of shooters had bagged eighteen brace of partridge.

In the days that are now long past the wives and daughters of the Lowton farmers had the reputation of being among the best cheese-makers in the county. It is said of one farmer who lived at Lowton Hall Farm, in conjunction with which he ran the village grocery stores, that he used to boast that anyone who lived on the bread and cheese made by his wife "Hud ne'er dee" (had never died) so efficacious did he claim these handicrafts of his wife to be.

This gentleman was a character in the village, and was known as "Fine Dickey" because of the peculiar verbosity of his speech, and his going about the village dressed in knee-breeches, swallow tailed coat and top hat, while his wife and two daughters were slaving on the farm and attending to the shop and their cheese and bread making.

The keeping of bees for the production of honey and wax has long been a home industry, and I find that as far back as the 16th August, 1670, an Ashton-in-Makerfield shop-keeper named Roger Lowe records the following in his diary:- "I borrowed a horse and went to Humphrey Burscoes at Lowton to buy some honey and wax off his sisters, but found them too hard for me." From the above it is apparent that more than 250 years ago the women of Lowton knew how to drive a hard

bargain, and there are those who say that this characteristic still prevails among the older generation of Lowtonians, for I have often heard it said that they always either "Win or set" in any transaction they enter into.

The old, picturesque, St Luke's Rectory, Lowton.

When I was a boy, my grandfather Ridyard had a dozen or more hives of bees, and I remember with what joy I hailed the time for squeezing the honey from the honeycombs a work in which I assisted him. On commencing our task, he always told me to eat as much honey as I cared to, and I thought what a kind and considerate grandfather he was. Of course I was soon satiated and it never entered my young mind that underlying his benevolence there was a sinister motive. He knew that if he allowed me to satisfy my longing I should afterwards pay more attention to squeezing out the honey from the combs.

In their season there was an abundance of flowers growing in the fields and hedgerows, from which the bees extracted the nectar with which to manufacture their honey. The Mayflower, buttercup, honeysuckle, wild rose, convolulus, the gorse shrub with its bright yellow flower, and many other varieties, scented the air with their sweet odour. In the spring-time the primrose adorned the copse and banks of of the then clear-running water brooks. Another of my youthful delights was gathering black-berries, and mushrooms of which there was often a plentiful supply during Autumn.

Prior to 1860 the educational facilities were poor, the only day schools in the village being a small one attached to St. Luke's Church, and a "Dame's" School kept by Betty Jolly in her cottage home near Lane Head. It is not surprising therefore that many of the inhabitants formed habits and modes of speech peculiarly their own.

In the "Leigh Monthly Magazine" published in 1844, a contributor writes as follows:-
"Perhaps there is no place in the vicinity of Leigh where the manners of the inhabitants have undergone a greater change within the last fourteen or fifteen years than Lowton Common. About that time nearly all were employed in muslin weaving, and as a manufacturer resided in the village, who found them all work, and as there were provision shops, etc. near, they had very little if any intercourse with Leigh. 'Saint Monday' used to be strictly kept, as there was scarcely a loom going on that day throughout the year.

In Summer it was usually spent in running, jumping, wrestling and fighting, and in Winter, in skating, kicking the football and other handy sports. It is not to be wondered at that they became proficient at these practices, and consequently let no opportunity slip of exhibiting their prowess. If they happened to come to Leigh during the fairs or other pastimes, it was generally in gangs of eight or ten, and many a piece of wanton mischief was committed, and many a bloody battle fought on those occasions. But the time had now arrived when silk was introduced into their workshops, and was the cause of an entire change in their habits. The pieces were so long that they could not finish them in a week and consequently had to work on Mondays the same as on other days. They

Long a popular hostelry for locals has been the Hare & Hounds, pictured in the early 20th century.

had likewise to attend the warehouse at Leigh with their work, hence a new familiar intercourse was generally generated and a kindlier feeling called forth between the workmen of the different neighbourhoods, and the bickerings and ill-blood have happily disappeared."

When I was a boy, I used to hear my elders speak of their past, and the above is a good description of the habits and customs of the inhabitants a hundred or more years ago, excepting that the writer does not include cock-fighting, which was prevalent in his list of pastimes. The practice of the rougher element of going in gangs to create trouble in the outlying districts did not die out until a much later period. Fifty years ago, running, jumping, and skating were still indulged in by many of the men and youths - myself included - living at Lowton Common end of the district, and several of the men used to advertise in a sporting paper called if I remember right "Bells Life" challenging competitors for a wager.

My own speciality was jumping by hops, and I remember that when I was about 18 years of age, covering 27¾ yards with six hops and a jump. There were, however, two other jumpers living in the village who could exceed that distance. Other forms of exercise indulged in by the youths of the district were 'Hare and Hounds' and 'Follow my Leader.' These forms of recreation were practised on winter moonlight nights, and I have run miles over the fields, hedges, and ditches in Lowton and Kenyon. I attribute my fairly long life and healthy constitution largely to these open air exercises indulged in and enjoyed during my young days.

Since the time of which I write the whole aspect of the district has changed. There was then no Lowton St. Mary's Railway Station or Bridge, but a number of stately elm and poplar trees, standing on both sides of the roadway of what are now the bridge and Station approaches. The highway was paved with cobble stones, and at Lane Head and Stone Cross Lane the toll-gates were still standing.

In the area extending from St. Mary's Church to the Parish boundary at Lowton Junction there were comparatively few houses, and excluding the Vicarage and Green Lane, few of them would be less than a century old, many of them considerably more. The old houses were mostly of one type, consisting of living-room, the floor of which was either flag or bricks, and "weaving shop" as the other ground floor room was usually called. The floor of this room was clay. The two bedrooms were open to the roof, which was either thatched with straw, or covered with thin flags. The walls of all the rooms were kept spotlessly clean by annual lime-washing. I believe there is only one thatched cottage in the Parish, the others having beeen taken down or re-roofed with modern slating. Time was when almost all of the old cottages were hives of industry muslin-weaving first being carried on in them, then silk weaving. When I was a boy there were very few houses in which there was not one or more looms in the earthen floor weaving shop.

Lowton St. Mary's Railway Station

In some, all the family were engaged in the business of weaving, and there could be heard the clickity-clack of two, three and sometimes four looms working harmoniously together. From the report of a census taken in 1865 of the number of hand-loom weavers in Leigh and district, I gather that out of a total of 3,129, Lowton is credited with having 190 males and 293 females engaged in the industry, a combined total of 483. Significantly the report states that 52 had left the business. For a considerable number of years steam power had been applied to work the looms engaged in weaving cotton, and had begun to be introduced to work the silk weaving loom. From this time hand-loom weaving began to decline and by 1890 it had almost become extinct in Lowton. In some respects this was to be regretted for families whose ancestors and themselves had made hand-loom weaving a fine art had to seek other means of earning a livelihood.

The average earnings of the weavers 90 or 100 years ago was miserably low being not more than ten shillings a week, out of which they paid a bobbin winder twenty or twenty-five per cent, leaving

Above Left: The Travellers Rest, one of the oldest inns in Lowton.
Right: One of Lowton's earliest taxi's with owner Jack Worsley, pictured in the 1930's. The Worsley's had previously provided a wagonette and landau service for visitors arriving at the local railway station.

their nett earnings seven or eight shillings per week. This was at a time, when as related to me by my grandmother Ridyard tea was 5/- per pound flour 3/6d per dozen lbs., and potatoes 2/6d per score lbs. She told how the people lived chiefly on jannock, treacle, oatmeal porridge and buttermilk, and she had known of children going round the village collecting potato peelings to boil and eat. A little meat and white bread at week ends was a luxury which only a few could afford. No wonder that some of the male weavers became embittered revolutionaries, and attributing the cause of their plight to the introduction of machinery, they joined the Chartist movement. a section of which went about the district demanding the stoppage of the mills under threat of drawing the safety plugs from the steam boilers.

For taking part in this extreme measure one of the Lowton weavers named George Bellamy was arrested and sent to prison for twelve months. Another man named Joseph Bromilow, whom I knew as an old man escaped arrest by hiding until he could safely set sail to America where he stayed for a few years. On his return to Lowton, he married a Miss Prescott, and a son of the marriage became manager of the old cotton mill which used to stand in Church Lane.

Most of the villagers being very poor and few able to read, they subscribed a half-penny each, weekly, with which to purchase a newspaper, which at the time cost eight pence each. During the week the subscribers congregated in one or other of the cottages to hear the news read aloud by a reader, the subject matter being then discussed. One of the best readers was a man named Birchall, who had a cottage school near by the old Methodist Chapel.

Almost all of the Lowton weavers have now passed away. The one however who wove the last piece of silk cloth executed in the village, is still living (1935). This is Mrs. Marsh, a widow who lives at "Pink Cottage" near Lowton St. Mary's Railway Station. I have known this lady all my life, and when I recently called upon her, we had a pleasant conversation reminiscent of our younger days. She informed me that it was in 1910 that she wove the cloth referred to in the shop of her present home on the request of the late Mr. George Hilton, by whom she was employed. This gentleman was the last of the hand-loom silk mercers in Leigh and district. He owned a small weaving shed near Leigh Canal Bridge, wherein he carried on business until his death, employing several weavers including Mrs. Marsh.

It was interesting to learn from Mrs. Marsh that she could earn by her weaving from 3/- to 5/- per day of 8 hours according to the class of work she had in hand, the price varying from sixpence to ten pence per yard. Out of this amount she paid her bobbin-winder two pence in the shilling. In their time these weavers had woven material for making the wedding dresses and lingerie for both English and foreign royalty, and also for other highly placed ladies at home and abroad.

The house in which my father was born is in a rather dilapidated condition, and is doomed to come down to make room for the contemplated new Council Schools, which are planned to be erected on the site. It looked like an old house when I was a boy, with its flagged roof, through which at times water percolated, and if it happened to be freezing, icicles formed during the night and hung over the beds in which my father and his young brothers were sleeping, and I have heard him say that he and his brothers have sucked the icicles as they lay in bed. Including my father, five brothers, and two sisters were reared in the house, and all of them lived to be over 70 years of age.

I remember several meetings being called to consider the question of an improved water supply. At the time the district depended on wells for drinking water, and on rain-tubs and ponds for washing and other domestic purposes. Although it was known that most of the wells were polluted, and some wells and ponds were at times dry, there was strong opposition to the scheme when it became known that it meant an increase of three pence per week rent and a slight increase in the rates. After several stormy meetings, wiser counsels prevailed, and a supply of tap water was carried to every house in the Parish.

Nurse Hayes was Lowton's midwife for almost fifty years and probably delivered babies to most homes in the village

One of the most strenuous opponents to the scheme was a man named Hindley, who owned a cottage in Church Lane. So bitter was he when the water was laid on to his house that every night before retiring to bed, he opened the tap allowing the water to run to waste. He was however, caught in the act. and had to appear before the magistrates at Leigh, who gave him a severe reprimand, and inflicted a heavy penalty for his foolhardy and antisocial conduct.

The village customs of 60 years ago have now fallen into decay. Barring out, or breaking up day for the Christmas holidays, was a great event for the boys attending St. Mary's School. On that day the older boys would early get possession of the school and fasten all the doors and windows. On the arrival of the teachers a note was handed to the head master informing him that there was no admittance unless he promised there would be no lessons but instead an immediate

Probably the only fresh water well remaining in Lowton pictured at Byrom's Farm

declaration that the school would be closed for a fortnght's holiday. To the delight of the scholars the teachers used to enter into the spirit and fun which the proceedings created. Mr. Heath was the first school master appointed when first it opened in 1862.

At Christmas time the living room of every cottage was adorned with evergreens gathered by the children from the hedgegrows in the district. On Shrove Tuesday these were taken down and I remember my mother religiously placing on the fire a piece of the holly, yew, or ivy, during the making of each pancake. The Sunday Schools and Churches were the centres of what social life there was in the Parish.

There was a good deal of drinking in the village in those days, particularly at week ends, many of the men spending most of their leisure time in the public houses, and some of the men occasionally went on the spree for as much as a week or a fortnight. There has however been a great change in this respect. It is obvious that 70 years ago the village was well supplied with drinking facilities, since there were no less than four breweries and ten public houses in the Parish, named as follows:- Travellers Rest, Red Lion, Kings Arms, Rams Head, Hare and Hounds, Jolly Carter, Church Inn,

17

This fascinating picture shows hundreds of local people preparing for a charabanc trip outside the King's Arms (formerly Queen's Arms) at Lane Head, Lowton, probably in the 1930's.

Shepherds Inn, Two Horse Shoes, and Three Horse Shoes. The houses with breweries attached were the Red Lion, Kings Arms, Rams Head. and Shepherds Inn. The Licences of the "Two and Three Horse Shoes" houses, as well as the breweries were done away with between 60 and 70 years ago.

Sixty years ago, the only means whereby the inhabitants could visit Leigh was on foot, and as the distance from Lane Head is about four miles, only the young and vigorous could undertake the journey. There was however little need for them to do so, as the village was fairly self contained with its several stores where food and almost all household requirements could be bought. There was also Sam Bate and his son Jemmy, the village tailors, who had the reputation of making corduroy suits and sleeved waistcoats second to none. George Howard, the cobbler, Joseph Taylor (otherwise Joe Clogger) who made and reclogged this, the then, popular footwear. There was also Dickey Yates, the village extractor of teeth the appearance of whose instruments of torture was sufficient to shock the nerves of the most troublesome tooth into quietude. Mr. Eden, the ladies dressmaker, and not the least important were the old dames who earned a precarious livelihood by knitting stockings, also mending and patching for the women weavers who had not the time to attend to these essential household requirements. The time came however when these home industries came to an end.

Mr. Worsley began to run an uncovered spring cart on Saturday afternoons, and plied for passengers. This venture proved a success, and in a short time he had two ramshackle waggonettes running, each making two journeys to and from Leigh. The patronage of the inhabitants which had previously gone to the local craftsmen and women, was transferred to Leigh shop-keepers, and these cottage industries ultimately came to an end. Mr. Worsley plied his vehicles until the electric trams compelled him to retire from the business more than thirty years ago.

One of Mr. Worsley's first and most regular passengers was a well known local character, named Mary Mee. She seldom failed to journey to Leigh and it was said she always arrived home a little bit 'forudish'. This lady was in great demand at births and deaths in the village. Her duties on a death taking place was to wash and lay-out the corpse and generally attend to the mourners on the day of the funeral with currant bread and wine, not forgetting to go round with a plate to recieve donations towards defraying the cost of the burial. Her temperament was such that she could laugh or cry just as the solemnity, or otherwise, of the occasion required.

DOLLY'S LANE AND BRIDGE

Winwick Lane which leads from Newton Road near the Chapel to Winwick, is best known to the older generation of Lowtonians as Dolly's Lane. When I was a boy the whole length of the Lane from a point a little beyond the old chapel was only a bridle path to the few farm houses and cottages abutting on to it. A few yards below the chapel there was a gate which was kept locked, and the key kept at the adjacent farm house. Before any vehicle could pass the gate the driver had to apply to the farm for the key and if his business extended beyond the end of the lane, he had to obtain permission to pass through.

How the Lane came to be called Dolly's was related to me many years ago by an old Lowtonian who worked on the Manchester-Liverpool railway during its construction. The line cuts through the lane near to several cottages, one of which was occupied at the time the line was made, by a family named Ridgeway. A grown up daughter was named Dorothy, who for abbreviation was called 'Dolly'. Having an eye to business, Dolly opened part of her home as a grocers shop, which in a short time developed into a veritable Lewis's store. Did the navvies want food or drink, tobacco, matches, shoelaces, buttons, thread, etc.. they soon found that Dolly could supply their requirements and her home-brewed herb beer was known to the men for its excellent quality for miles along the line. Kind and obliging in disposition, she attended to the navvies' cuts and bruises with the adhesive plaster she sold, and with concoctions made from the herbs she grew in her garden, their bodily ailments were eased. Needless to say she won the mens hearts, and they looked up to her as their fairy godmother and she was no doubt the subject of much of their daily conversation.

In memory of her, they named the lane in which she lived 'Dolly's Lane' and the bridge over the railway near her home 'Dolly's Bridge'. By this name the lane and bridge have been known for a hundred years, but in recent times the old Lane has been modernized and named Winwick Lane by an unromantic District Council.

What a wonderful atmospheric photograph this is of Kenyon Lane, showing the old smithy on the left in the 1920s. The scene has changed very little even to this day

Two

On the morning of Tuesday, September 18th, 1883, the inhabitants of Lowton Common were jolted from their usual composure by a report that Joshua Rigby, a well-known local farmer, had been found dead in his bedroom with his throat cut. The circumstances surrounding the tragedy, concerning which I have a vivid recollection, are as follows:

Mr. Rigby was tenant of Cheetham Fold Farm, situated near to the Jolly Carter Inn, and although 73 years of age, he was a strong and vigorous man. He was a bachelor, and for many years had living with him, two maiden sisters, one of whom had died a year or so previous to the tragic end of her brother.

Mr. Rigby had the unenviable reputation among the villagers of being a hard task-master, bad tempered, and particularly unmerciful in his conduct towards his aged sisters, and he was spoken of in the district as being a bad and 'nowty mon'; in fact it was rumoured on the death of his sister that she came to an untimely end because of his brutality towards her. There also lived at the farmstead a nephew, named John Gibbons, who managed the farm for his uncle who shortly after the death of his aunt, married a Lowton young woman named Martha Bent, it having been previously arranged that after their marriage both should dwell at the farm. There was at the time another nephew, named after his uncle, Joshua Rigby, and was known locally as 'Young Jash'. He occasionally assisted on the farm, and lived with his wife and family in the cottage, still standing opposite the gateway leading down to the farm.

Old Joshua was possessed of considerable wealth, and had often boasted in the "Jolly Carter" of having money in several banks, and it was common knowledge that he used to threaten his nephews, according to how one or the other pleased him, or displeased him, that he would leave his money to the other. A few weeks before the old man was found dead he was seen beating his sister with the buckle end of his leather strap when the nephew, Joshua, intervened, and threatened to report his uncle's brutal conduct to the police. In his rage he ordered Joshua off the premises, and his sister left to live with Gibbons' mother, who resided at Leigh. Afraid that he would end his days in prison for cruelty to his sister, the old man was prevailed upon by Gibbons, so it was said, to make his will in his favour, making him sole legatee and executor.,,

Mr. Page, the village schoolmaster, was sent for and instructed by the old man, drew up the following will:-

This is the last Will and Testament of me Joshua Rigby of Lowton in the County of Lancaster, farmer. I hereby give and devise and bequeath to my nephew John Gibbons, his heirs, executors and administrators for his and their own use and benefit absolutely and for ever, all my estate and effects, both real and personal whatsoever and wheresoever, and of what nature and quality soever, and I hereby appoint him, the said John Gibbons, sole executor of this my Will. In Witness whereof I have hereunto set my hand this second day of June, One thousand eight hundred and eighty-three. Joshua Rigby.

Signed by the said Joshua Rigby in the present of us present at the same time, who in his presence and in the presence of each other, attest and subscribe our names as witnesses hereto. George Howard, Boot-maker, Lowton; Thomas Bent, Silk Weaver, Lowton.

The above in brief was the position in that unhappy household down to Sunday, September 9th, nine days before the murder. During the afternoon on this day, Mrs. Gibbons, cleaned the kitchen floor after which she went upstairs to wash and change her dress, leaving Mr. Rigby sitting in his armchair. On coming down, she found several hens walking about on her newly cleaned floor, and she blamed the old man for permitting them to enter the kitchen. In retaliation he got a pail of dirty water and dashed it over the floor. Outraged by his conduct, Mrs. Gibbons packed up some of her belongings and went to the home of her parents, who lived near by declaring she would never go back to the farm so long as the old man was there. During the days which followed, Gibbons slept at the farm, and in the meantime endeavoured to persuade his wife to go back to the farm, but she was against any such proposal.

On the Monday evening preceeding the murder, he was with his wife at her parents home, leaving her about midnight. On arriving at the farm be found the door locked, and concluding that his uncle had gone to bed, he decided not to disturb him, but would snatch a few hours in the barn. He was up early the following morning and went about his work feeding and milking the cows. etc. While he was attending to these duties, two farm labourers, respectively named Richardson and Bent, had put in an appearance, and were busy stacking a load of hay, which had been gathered the previous day. On seeing Gibbons come out of the shippon the men shouted to him asking where the old man was, knowing that it was his custom to be out and about the farm yard.

Gibbons asked if they had not seen him knocking about yet and said "I will go and see". He found the kitchen door still locked, and he then went round the house to a small window on the ground floor which he knew was never fastened. On getting into the house he shouted, but receiving no reply he went upstairs, and found his uncle lying on the bedroom floor, near his bed, besmeared with blood, and dead. On his coming out of the house seemingly distressed the men asked what was the matter, and again asked where the old man was.

Gibbons replied that he was where he would stay until he was carried down, implying that his uncle was dead. Astounded with the news, they went with Gibbons to see the body, which they lifted on to the bed, their impression being that the old man had committed suicide by cutting his throat, and in falling, had made a severe wound on the head by it coming in contact with the door-post. While Gibbons went to inform the local policeman of what had happened. a woman named

Battersby had been called in to wash and lay out the body, and by the time Superintendent Jackson, and Inspector Dunn arrived on the scene from Leigh, all the clothes with blood on them had been washed, and the body laid on the bedroom door, which had been taken from its hinges, for the purpose. Gibbons, Richardson, Bent, and Mrs. Battersby, were closely questioned by the police, and on a search warrant being issued, the Will and bank books were found in a coat pocket belonging to Gibbons, hanging behind a door at his wife's parents' home. Gibbons was arrested and brought before F.W. Bouth, a magistrate at Leigh Police Court, on the Wednesday, and remanded on suspicion.

The inquest was held at the "Jolly Carter Inn", the Coroner being T. W. Barker, and the following jurymen:- W. Page, Schoolmaster, foreman of the jury; Henry Boydell, Silk-weaver; W. Marsh, Weaver; James Ince, Grocer; Richard Battersby, Weaver; James Turton, Weaver; George Marsh, Weaver; Peter Hesford, Night Watchman at Knott's Mill; Richard Eckersley, Clerk at Knott's Mill; James Pollitt, Gentleman; Henry Penkethman, Farmer; George Howard, Bootmaker. Mr. Cobbett, barrister, of Manchester appeared on behalf of the Treasury, Drs. Perrin and Brideoak, had made a post-mortem examination of the body, and Dr. Campbell Brown, County Analyst, gave evidence of having examined the prisoner's clothes and boots.

Gibbons was present at the inquest, and as the witnesses gave evidence of the incidents I have recorded, and the doctors' statement that in their examination of the body, they found, besides the throat having been cut, various marks on the arms and chest made by a sharp instrument, and the wound on the head had been made by something blunt and could have been caused by the heavy boots worn by the prisoner the case against Gibbons seemed very black indeed. Especially when Dr. Campbell Brown gave evidence to the effect that he had found a grey hair 2 inches long in the seam of prisoner's right boot, which undoubtedly had come from the dead man's head.

The jury having considered their verdict, the foreman, Mr. Page, read the following:- "We unanimously find that the deceased, Joshua Rigby, was murdered by being struck on the head by some heavy instrument, and we agree that there is sufficient evidence to have John Gibbons tried at a superior court." The Coroner then said:- "That is a verdict of Wilful Murder against John Gibbons". Gibbons was ordered to stand up, and the Coroner addressing him said "I am obliged to commit you to the next Assizes at Liverpool to take your trial on the indictment charging you with wilful murder." Gibbons was then removed in custody to Strangeways Jail, Manchester.

On Wednesday, October 17th, he was charged at Leigh Police Court with the wilful murder of his uncle on the 18th September. He was defended by a well-known Bolton solicitor named Richardson, who was nicknamed, 'Fat Dick' by frequenters of the Police Courts because of his tall and slim proportions. Mr. Cobbett, barrister of Manchester, represented the Treasury. I was present at the trial, and it was very interesting to listen to Mr. Richardson turn what seemed incriminating evidence in his client's favour. However, at the end of the day's proceedings the magistrates committed the prisoner to Kirkdale Jail, Liverpool, to await trial on the charge of murdering his uncle.

On Monday, November 18th. he was brought before Mr. Justice Denman and Jury at Liverpool Assizes. Mr. Shee and Mr. J. W. Lowther, instructed by Mr. Cobbert, were the prosecuting counsel, and Mr. Atkinson, with Mr. Wharton, instructed by Mr. Richardson, appeared for the defence. At the trial Mr. Atkinson used the same arguments, and adopted a similar line of defence that Mr. Richardson used at Leigh Police Court. During the afternoon one of the jury men was suddenly taken ill and had to retire, which incident brought the proceedings for the day to a close. On the following day, the juryman being still too sick to appear, the judge and counsel had a private consultation, after which the judge advised a verdict of not guilty stating that on the evidence advanced, no jury would convict.

Thus ended the only trial for murder ever brought against a Lowton inhabitant. During his two months incarceration, Gibbons put on 30 lbs. in weight, and on his return to the village, on Tuesday evening, he looked the picture of health. The Leigh Chronicle published a special edition, containing a full report of the trial, which was bought by the villagers like the proverbial hot cakes. Naturally, the murder trial, was the principal topic of conversation at Lowton Common for a long time. and many were the weird reports circulated of the murdered man's ghost having been seen stalking about the then lonely lanes and fields during the Winter nights.

A VISIT TO SOUTHPORT

Our annual and favourite Summer resort was Southport, which I remember as a very small place, and the promenade only reaching from Coronation Walk to Neville Street. We used to go with our luggage in a cart to Plank Lane, then embarking on the swift Packet at 11am, at the rate of 6 miles an hour, and after many enjoyable incidents on the voyage down the canal, would arrive at Scarisbrick at 6pm, then a scramble for a conveyance, which if missed, had to walk about 6 miles. The principal attractions and amusements at Southport 50 years ago, were riding on donkeys to low water, or the 'New Inn', gathering shells, bathing from caravans, sailing in small boats, no pier, no baths, no Winter Gardens, no Cambridge, etc., etc.

RECOLLECTIONS OF PEOPLE I HAVE MET WITH IN LOWTON, AND THEIR SAYINGS AND FASHIONS

Old Billy Turner, who worked for my father and grandfather, upwards of 50 years, used to delight in telling us (when children) all kinds of stories about boggarts, witches, and such like, enough to make our hair stand on end, like the quills on a fretful porcupine. On Sundays we used to read to him all the most horrible stories out of Fox's Book of Martyrs, on purpose to see him cry, and stroke his hand across his face saying:- 'Gosh, thoos were hard tiomes'. He was often at work at 4am until 8 or 9 in the evening. He appreciated anyone who gave him anything in the way a tip, and would say, "Thats o raal gentlemon" or "thats ah weel browt up lady". If no kind rememberance he would say, "He or she is goot nowt". Such is human nature.

"Old John Clayton (Alias Doll Rags) who used to attend all the funerals of Lowtonians who were interred at Winwick, walking in procession, and putting on for the nonce a very mournful and lugrubrious cast of countenance. No waggonettes, or shillibeers in those days, cakes and ale served out at 'The Swan', and a collection from the mourners to defray expenses. He also used periodically to walk as far as Warrington, six miles, and buy a pennyworth of needles. These were grand holiday tours, and full of enjoyment, and the incidents and adventures for some time to time, being as the poet says, 'the simple annals of the poor'.

Truncheons for the Parish constable were bought, a new lock purchased for the village stocks, and a halfpenny per head for thousands of sparrows was paid. I had often wondered where the boulderstones used for paving the highway previously mentioned were carted from and in one of the documents I found that they were brought to Winwick Quay in barges along the Sankey Canal, which joins with the River Mersey. This canal was opened in 1755 and the construction of the highway commenced eight or ten years later. The price for carting stones and other material was two shillings per day for a man with horse and cart. The paving ballast was carted from the various sand pits in the district.

It is interesting to know that previous to the Workhouse being opened in 1818, the paupers were sent to the Warrington Institution, which was then situated at Grappenhall, the Lowton Overseers being charged twopence halfpenny per day for the maintenance of each inmate sent by them.

For minor offences against the law, such as drunkenness or brawling, the delinquents were placed in the village stocks, but for more serious offences they had to appear before the magistrates at the Warrington Police Court. Like many of the Lancashire villages situated near industrial centres, Lowton has undergone vast changes during the past 60 years. From being an isolated and scattered Township governed by overseers and church wardens, it now forms part of Golborne Urban District, the inhabitants being represented on the Council by their chosen triennially elected councillors.

The new East Lancashire Road has obliterated many of the landmarks known to me in my youthful days. the houses and population have more than doubled in number, and the once dark, cobblestone highways have been tar-macadamised and electrically lighted, and now compare favourably with the best constructed highways in the County. The district is well served with facilities for travel, both by train and 'bus, and during my lifetime its topography has completely changed. It may be said that in writing these memoirs I look upon Lowton with partial eyes. If so, I make no apology, for there are few who do not cherish affection for the spot that gave them birth, no matter where it may be.

A Photo Album

Posing for the photographer, as they prepare for a popular charabanc trip in the 1920s, were these parishioners from St Luke's Church in Lowton

**Lowton Brass Band, nicknamed the 'Buttermilk Band' is pictured
in this busy scene in the early years of the 20th century**

How times have changed! This was a competitor in a ploughing match using a single furrow plough

A crowd enjoys the scene as a local farmer takes his turn in the local ploughing match sometime in the 1930s.

**Byrom's Farm,
Newton Road, Lowton.**

**Threshing corn in the days
prior to the combine
harvester was a long job,
and threshing machines
travelled from farm to farm
as they were needed**

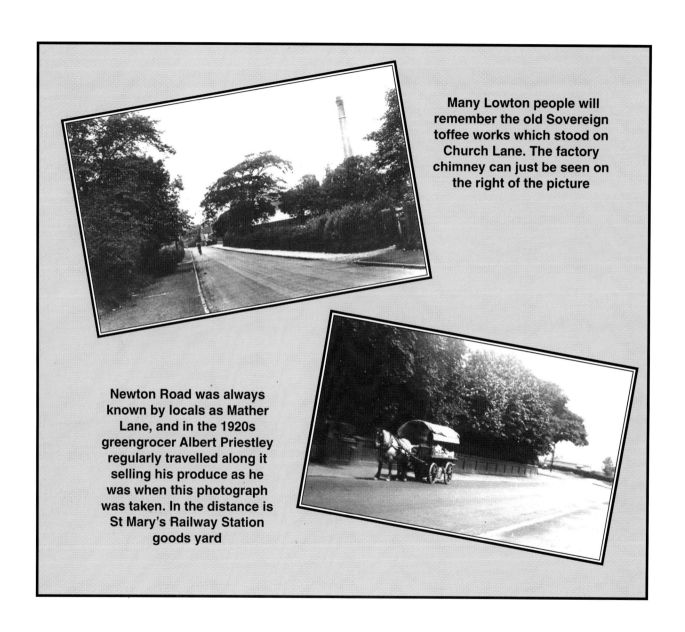

Many Lowton people will remember the old Sovereign toffee works which stood on Church Lane. The factory chimney can just be seen on the right of the picture

Newton Road was always known by locals as Mather Lane, and in the 1920s greengrocer Albert Priestley regularly travelled along it selling his produce as he was when this photograph was taken. In the distance is St Mary's Railway Station goods yard